This Close

Karen Klein

Copyright © 2022 Karen Klein
Copyrights for individual poems are
held by the authors

Ibbetson Street Press
25 School Street
Somerville MA 02143

www.ibbetsonpress.com

All rights reserved including the right to reproduce this work
in any form except as provided by U.S. Copyright law.
For information contact the publisher.

ISBN 978-1-4357-6452-1

Cover art by Kathryn Wolfson
Book design by S.R. Glines
text & titles: Caslon Pro

Contents

the curvature   of a line

Journal 2017: Bilbao	5
Takeoff	6

skin/has its own/vocabulary

Terra Nova	9
Parthenon	11
Jumper	13
Black Iris	14
You there	16
The Other Side	17
Yom Kippur	19
12/31	20
Oh, Those Men	21
'Froggie Went a Courtin'	23
Hunger	24
Alphabet Soup	25

use words   to find my tribe

Scribble	29
Tribal Tongues	30
Little Twinkie Toes	31
Night Lights	32
indigo	34
Shostakovich 5th	35

They won't come back next year

Hearing the Borromeo Quartet Play Beethoven's "Heiliger Dankgesang"	39
Marking Time	41
Glynnis Falls Park	43
Cicada Summer	44
Naps	45
Raspberry Patch	46
Shower	50
Journal 2017: Cordoba	51
Wild Swans at Waquoit	54
gut knowledge	56
Planted	57
Sequoia	58
October Rose	59

road to nowhere/and everywhere

Commitment to Poetry	63
My Orion	64
Thermometer	65
When We Could Still Go Home	66
The Rite of Spring	67
Spring	69
'the green fuse'	70
Acknowledgments	71
About the Author	75

This Close

the curvature of a line

Journal 2017: Bilbao

to walk on Santiago Calatrava's bridge
is to walk on a wish
to be free of rectangles
is to honor the architect's desire
to be a curve
suspended in space

it's a memory of a swing
the seat pulled way back
in a strong arc
the moment I am ready
then stretch my legs way out
to pump

the excitementof reaching

Takeoff

in bronze
polished by the artist himself
to the gleam of a freshly washed face
bouncing light
a revelation
solid heaviness   Brancusi's bird
caught in flight

seventeen in New York City
for the first time
in MoMA
for the first time

see the sculpture
—my breath catches itself—
the free curvature of our bodies
without an image of a body
the desired roundness of flesh
embodied

in the curvature of a line

skin/has its own/vocabulary

Terra Nova

We knew we had to say good-bye,
but didn't know how.
Me, thirteen; Mike, fifteen,
summer's end nineteen-fifty.

It wasn't really a romance;
we hung with the group,
not a couple, but an unspoken
awareness that we *liked* each other.

Here he is on the front steps,
going home to California tomorrow.
Light from the household through the screen
door as the evening advances.

We float in a lake of awkward.
Maybe he told me about his parents'
impending divorce which brought him
to Fargo to summer with his grandma.

Probably we reminisced about the lake
in Minnesota where we waterskied
on surfboards across the wake
as his cousin drove the swerving speedboat.

This is not a date; no plans for future meetings.
Our bodies knew what we wanted,
but couldn't speak it. Suddenly aware
of the increasingly late hour, we listen.

10

I had played spin-the-bottle before,
but that was just a game. This is not a game.
Inevitably, like bobbing corks,
we collide into the first real kiss for both.

I didn't sleep all night,
riveted between exhilaration and fear.
My new body had crossed
into unknown, raw territory.

No way back. The Angel held her flaming
sword barring my way to yesterday's me.
Now in danger forever, someday
I would walk into it naked.

Parthenon

from Ellinikon to Athens the bus
driver gently navigates
3am dark
the road so familiar

not familiar to me, first time tourist
the night too profound
for glimpses of habitation
or signs in a script
I can't read

bus windows
sudden burst of
surprising brilliance
the Parthenon illuminated
rises out of darkness
dominates the surround

my eyes follow as long as I can
the iconic image   its pillars
so weighted with horror and truth
only stones can hold its legacy
familiar to me through college
classroom filters

dramas, epics, politics
the old family stories:
desire, vengeance, blood
going to war, *nostos*, coming home

Woman, who moved my bed?

longing for a shared bed
a bond intense as theirs
is my Odysseus still wandering
or am I Odysseus
wandering alone
on his turf

Jumper

Horns of the Bull   their lyrical curve
swoops upward   reaches a murderous point
our lyres echo their shape

I stand in front   a slave in Minoan Crete

The Bull sits   waits   eyes me
two trainers   one at each end   their command
grab the horns flip upward over Him stick the landing

Where does fear live in a body

My people taken generations ago   Thera destroyed
by volcanic horror   homeland ashes scattered to Minoans
we serve the Bull   worshipped in Knossos

He will not sit   at the ritual performances
my small bare breasts still budding
rush towards Him   arms stretched straight

Eager hands clasp His horns   fleeting merge
of two bodies   my bent knees   stamp the Earth
jump

Feet skyward   spine arch
my whole body opens   outward
into convex circle's perfect arc

Feel the Aegean sun   bathe me golden

Black Iris
for Georgia O'Keefe

after I saw it
could not see anything else

walked out of the Metropolitan Museum

walked naked to myself
recognized my body in the flower
the iris intimately in me
knew I could say cunt
knew it was good

lush outer labial petals
of the purple to indigo iris
tender inner petals
the color of blood
mixed to a pink wash

hidden clitoral remnant
protected by upper closing folds
our curious vaginal recess
mine and O'Keefe's
too dark to decipher

could finally name the names
forbidden and unspoken
to the child I was
when 'down there' meant
everything my hands should
never touch, nor anyone else's

his fingers
my hair
iris opening

You there

at low tide
the stones just sharp enough
to hurt my feet
if I walk too fast
not big enough to do damage
but enough rough edges
to make me think first
before placing my foot

a small irritation
enough to disturb my sleep
like the princess who felt the pea
under twenty mattresses
--or was it forty—
like the sound of your voice
its memory grown fainter these many years
gravelly with desire
saying my name

The Other Side

I.
When you split wood,
one side knows
it belongs to what it has lost

the ache to rejoin
its juncture
an open sore.

Scar tissue
is always
second best.

II.
Split wood
its uneven edges
retain slivers.

Without loyalty
betrayal
has nothing to eviscerate.

Without the possibility
of betrayal
loyalty remains rhetoric.

III.
The other side
of silence
is not emptiness.

Giacometti said
"one must try…
to translate one's sensations."

Skin
has its own
vocabulary.

Yom Kippur

The day eats itself;
sunless light leaves no
markers for the passage
of the hours.

I think of the horses
drawing Apollo's chariot
hidden in their cloudy
shroud. Do they gallop, amble,
wildly stumble their way across
the sky? Does their day seem
as endless as my thoughts

excavating old grievances
their stinging mercurochrome
the places I was
the places I was not
peeling off the pretend face
hiding shame,
taking out guilt's nettle
from its pus-filled core
putting it back in

again.

12/31

sitting home, two friends, divorcees
with no dates to kiss at midnight
and one restless bored pre-teen
with nothing to do
we decide to go skating

waning gibbous moon still large enough
to bring skyshine to a frozen suburban
pond surrounded by bare oak branches
and New England's evergreens
to connect the pond's shallow luminosity
to its moonself
to create between them an enchanted barrier
keeping out the rest of the world

pond vacant   just us three in moonlight
and thick, inviting ice   promising safety
bladed   we glide into liberating movement

traveling wherever   round   and around   round
                free
sometimes solo turns
sometimes grab hands   tug together

never repeated   never forgotten

Oh, Those Men
a list poem

I have lost six of you in five years.
I haven't really lost you.
I just don't know where to find you.

Reciting a list of your names becomes
a trochaic chant in chronological death order:
Stephen
    Marvin
        Jimmy
            Louie
                Richard
                    Donald

I would conjure Stephen's hospitality
the whiskey Marvin brought to drink all night
    Jimmy's jokes
        the books Louie gave me
            Richard's hand so like his mother's
                the annual birthday card from Donald:
                    'No matter how old you are,
                        I'll always be a year younger'

Yesterday a beach day for the books,
summer suspended in non time.
Warm water in Vineyard Sound,
the coquettish slap of the waves
pulling us in to wallow in pleasure.

I wanted the day to last forever,
to go back to the house, towels flying,
for endless glasses of red, to make
steamers and drown them in butter,
to talk til the cow jumped over the moon.

When he claimed the highest form of love
is friendship, Aristotle's insight was audaciously
perceptive. But when he restricted this friendship
to that between men, he was way off the mark.
He had a lot to learn.

'Froggie Went a Courtin'
for Jennifer M. memories of a happy day

Water at the pond's edge
a seething cauldron
eccentrically round shapes
bubble into air
fall into water
not bubbles
frenzied frogs
pushing
attacking
fleeing
clinging
stuck pairs
orgiastic chaos
males open their mouths
so wide it hides their bodies
an obscene darkness
emits repetitive echoes
the raspy burps
harsh monotony of brrrrrrrrp

Mesmerized, we wonder
does desire have a role?
is it all instinct ?

Two frogs discretely separated settle in a line
facing us directly; their button-dark eyes stare
fixedly   rebuking our presence:
our ritual is not a spectator sport

Hunger

We meet in the street   I want
to invite you in for tea   but
can't   neither vaccinated

Winter hangs on   cat's claws
on a ledge   dirty snow patches   drear chill
our warm coats   you with your bicycle

Seasons slow turning   you come in
afternoon teas   wine and cheese at dusk
brief touch   my shoulder   your hand

Scilla   daffodils   crocus   petals
opening everywhere   first big hug
our octopus arms

touch through layers
two old   clothed bodies
I want to stay held and to hold

Now my bones know
how much   how long
I've missed a You

Alphabet Soup

As a kid I ate a lot,
remember it now as thick
with macaroni letters my spoon chases,
trying to corner a "K"
and capture the rest to spell my name.
No memory of its taste.
I didn't think of it as food.
It was my lunch time game.

Alone in a bed built for two,
trying to snag sleep
from the alphabet soup of lovers,
the pleasurable memories I float in,
I remember the letters of their names—
well not all last names, some initials—
their bodies, their hands on me,
onset of the sharp, unexpectedly
wild cunt-brain connection.
Drowsing toward sleep, still
float on the memory soup
of good sex.

use words   to find my tribe

Scribble

the straightest line in Kaethe Kollwitz'
self-portrait
runs from the artist's eye to the fingers
holding the charcoal
intention's arrow   hitting its mark

other marks   curved   smudged
softness in the perfectly articulated
face   barely noticed   beside
the eruption of her crayon's side   wide
jagged   unbroken diagonals

one instantaneous swoop of elbow   wrist
continuous up down   up down   up
obliterates the already drawn   arm
that holds the hand   fingers   tool
this gestural violence   brings

her impulsive dance of rage
frustration at her failure
to create the illusion
of the right arm's
three-dimensions

or just spontaneous physicality
breaking free of formal artistic
restraints   smashing patterns
of what's allowed what's not
Kaethe Kollwitz enters her art work

Tribal Tongues

I don't have one. My dad did
his native English included
meshugenah, meshugah, meshugos
words containing infinite nuances
from mildly eccentric to stupid
from foolish to dangerously nutty
words from a language his family
repudiated   his Jewish mother's phrase
for Jews she disdained as 'too Yiddish'.

Mother's native tongue too attenuated
and hidden to share with her children
the coffee pot, always hot, waited for one
of her six sisters to come for gossip
laments   grievances in the language
of their illiterate Norwegian parents
ooftah the sound of breath expelled
when you put down a heavy child
or lift an unwelcome load   and *feedah*
strongly stressed on the first syllable
the sound of repugnance at the stench
of lutefish cooking in the basement
only at Christmas.

I inherit tribal echoes growing fainter
over the years   rummage through English
use words   to find my tribe
those *meshugah* enough to make poems.

Little Twinkie Toes
A.M.W. 1/7/1900- 4/14/1993

My mother loved Elvis.
Coming from Manhattan to Mashpee
she'd pour a slug of Bailey's Irish Cream
and close the door to her room.
Sounds of gospel rock and cigarette smoke
let us know she'd settled in.

My mother loved to dance
but she married a man who loved
gin rummy and schmoozing.
She lived a long time after he died.
After dinner, she'd tap dance in her little silver shoes
singing "They called the lady Louisville Lou."

My mother loved puzzles.
A permanently set up card table held
a jumble of pieces. Their jigsaws
found partners and over weeks
a landscape emerged. The puzzle complete,
she penciled answers in stacks of crosswords.

My mother's dream was to be on TV.
She saw an old woman in an ad that she made
famous "Where's the beef?" and thought
I can do that. My sister got her a head shot.
She went to a cattle call, panicked at the mob,
refused to audition, and walked away from fame.

Wrong move, Ma. If you'd auditioned, you'd
still be on TV hawking someone's product,
and I'd still be able to see and to hear you.

Night Lights

I.

above me
Perseid Showers
evanescent smears
ignite the night
I watch for hours

II.

drowning in the sky
come up for breath
cling to Cassiopeia—the big W
Pleiades—the seven sisters
saying their names Merope   Alcyone
Electra   over and over
as if by giving them names
by speaking from our star
I'll find my bearings
where I have no home

III.

remember a carnival at night
rotating ferris wheel lights
the flicker of the tilt-a-whirl
round-a-bout carousel shadows
my mother and Tante Hans
brought me   I'm five   small
lost in a moving crowd
a fence of legs I can't get through
scared   screaming
want my mother   want to tell her
my stomach aches

IV.

another plunge
into fireworks' universe
come up gasping
for language I don't have
for words I don't know
for words that may not even exist
to describe enormity
the tumble of a speck

indigo

seduced me   it could not have been the sound
of the word   Mother's spirit in an evening gown
plush indigo velvet bodice   for in dreams sounds

are intuited   perhaps the tripartite process
of monosyllables   mime the brevity of her appearance
swirling chiffon skirt   coming in only to go out

the tongue caresses the teeth lips nearly closed   *in*
I never saw her wear indigo
then the jaw widens as the tongue gives

preferring muted plant greens   sage   olive
a quick pat to the teeth and lowers itself
the lips move gently apart   *di*

finally the jaw drops lips tighten   protrude
pull into a soft cushy babycircle   nippleready   *go*
the choreography of the mouth

Shostakovich 5th

Strings pounce on the note,
startle the audience to attention.
We didn't know what was coming.
We didn't know we would drown.
We will drown.

through the tumult of horns
a solo instrument
sometimes a violin   sometimes a flute
the ache of its melody
a stiletto thrust that opens memory's wounds and weeps
my baby sister, snowblonde, running after Skippy, her little legs churning

peppy march
stomping along with its brutal irony
wave after wave   flute   oboe   cello
pulls us out

woman in front of me, hunched over
fists clenched/unclenched
arms pulse up and down

undertow drags us back within
steam tent   her congested coughing
clear celeste harp tones
wrench tangled knots of childhood
old parental voices   *the squeaky wheel gets the grease*

tympani boils over
cymbals slash through brass blare
we give in
we give up
we beg
the composer begs
for release
from old   unresolvable   contradictions

Exhausted silence.

Then like a giant breaker the audience
rises.

Roars.

They won't come back next year

Hearing the Borromeo Quartet Play Beethoven's "Heiliger Dankgesang"

I. First, the chords.

Their sound humbles adjectives --
stately, sonorous, majestic, resonant--
exposes the words' inadequacy.

The measured progression
hones our attention,
makes us wait, expectant.

The diapason calls forth the presence
of an absent organ, as if it were the instrument
not a mere string quartet.

II. Then, the melodic phrase.

It enters with full humility
through the second violin,
the first too grand for its modest approach.

Yet it returns again, plaintive, and again,
its repetitive insistence like a child's why
that never gets an answer.

III. Finally, the melodic phrase.

This time in the first violin—its timbre firm,
Beethoven after his near-fatal illness,
the composition a product of his recovery.

But this is no "holy song of thanks."
The certitude he brought back
becomes an urgent plea

that when the Dark Angel closes in,
his wings will obliterate fear,
his embrace be compassionate.

Marking Time

I.

Words for wanting
contain 'L':
lonely
garrulous
old.
To make the sound
your tongue touches
the top of your palate
leaving a little space beneath
for moisture
to pool
like the still pools
of water
in hollow places
after rain.

II.

"Hair is like a fingerprint"
she snipped during cut to curl
when I complained my left side
curls, my right side doesn't.

Imagine fingerprint whorls
in hair patterns and toeprints,
our print-filled bodies complex
as Tibetan mandalas, Aboriginal dream paintings.

III.

At first glance, a bird, then I saw a jaw, teeth, bones of hip, spine,
no flesh or fur,
only a skeleton lodged in fallen leaves in the wilder verge of my
land.
What brought this small animal there for final rest?
a hunter? a coyote?
or just wild seeking wild?

Glynnis Falls Park

The dead deer at the entrance,
maybe it was there all along,
the greedy flies clustered
at its sweet underbelly
its vulnerable, young penis.
Its head flung back,
the arched curve of its neck
a reflexive response to the blow
of the exiting car that didn't register the hit,
or if it did, sped away anyway.

The park pathway littered
with leaves, still a few trees holding green,
the gentle transition to a more bitter time,
an unhurried waiting for the icy winds,
the ravaging storms which left their marks
of past damage in downed trees' mammoth trunks.

As we amble along the trail, the dog at our side,
we anticipate the casserole simmering
in the slow cooker, comfort food for fall,
beans from the farmers market's last harvest.
Even nature acquiesces in this calm acceptance
of inevitable endings. We're almost ready
to accept our own.
                      But the Airedale rushes ahead,
flings his back down on the leaves. Paws raised,
he wriggles in ecstasy, leaps up to roll in the next leaf
pile with the exuberant joy, the vitality of animal spirits.

Cicada Summer
For Elva, 1/1937-6/2021, with love

On the oaks
random patches of brown leaves
dead where the cicada lived
their orgiastic three days
of mating & flying & mating & dying.
These sere brown do not fall off,
but stay next to the fulsome green
with no discernible pattern.

Would it help to imagine
our brains like this ------
an oak tree, a hodgepodge
of live and dead memories
stored side by side?
The brown ones are lost to us,
yet they're there, souvenirs
of the life we once had.

Was I still in one of your
green leaves?

Naps

Grown-ups like to take naps.
Kids don't.

I'm a grown-up.
I don't like to take naps.
I'm afraid of them.

It's not a fear of putting
my sleep cycle out of order.
It's older, deeper.

I don't remember my exact age
when it happens, probably fourteen or so.
I remember my bedroom, the floral pillowcases.

I fell asleep during daylight.
When I awoke, it was night.
To say it was terrifying,
or to say I was in terror
implies that I was thinking.
I wasn't thinking.
It was thinking me.
I knew I would die.
I knew I would wake in the dark.

Raspberry Patch
fragments vital for the understanding of the whole   Wm Kentridge

I.

1225 Ninth Street South   Fargo, North Dakota
gathering place for *'The Wilk Family of Tilsit'*
cousins&siblings   close&distant from all the States
of their exilic American homes   reunions of those
who came out of East Prussia in time
my memory of survivors' names   so many Harry's

Furniture too large for the rooms   heavy chairs
too big for me   an immigrants' house
we eat our main meal   here midday
rich soup with meat-filled kreplach
Grandma and Tante Hans rolling dough
roasting meat, potatoes, carrots
--at home ice cream for dessert--   not here
anyway I'm already   full

Grandpa Wilk always in the enveloping
chair wrapped in afghans Grandma knit
his aging body always cold   always bronchial
holding loss

We children went to the Synagogue, but the Lord
 closed his ears to our prayer…Mother left [four] sons
 and[one] daughter to mourn…I the oldest [thirteen and a half]
 …. This ends my childhood….

I'm the granddaughter from his Christian
daughter-in-law his only son's daughter   sitting
at his feet   his wildly blue eyes
"Don't let them tell you the Jews killed Jesus."

behind the house   a secret place
for a five year old   thickets and thorns
little fingers reach to pluck   red sweetness
berries redden my mouth   small punctures
scratches redden my skin   densely tangled
raspberry patch   no path but desire

II.

Rosa&Louis Wilk d. Kazlu Ruda, Lithuania 1941
Leo Wilk d. Riga Ghetto, Latvia   1/1942
Gertrude Wilk d. 9/1942 Ruth Wilk d. 10/1942 Treblinka, Poland
Harry Wilk d. 7/1944 Theresienstadt, Czechoslovakia

Too many relatives come to Fargo
overwhelmed by adult multitudes
my tantrum exiled to the garden
with a flower whose fuschia blossoms
on different strands   wave a bit with
breezy motions   fascinate me   motionless
flowers that bloom down not up
staring at them calms me
Grandma Wilk says Bleeding Hearts

Treasure from Tilsit, a cloisonné teapot
inlaid flowers and bluebirds
my make-believe parties with that teapot

their early days of marriage
we lived like two doves in a nest…
Henrietta a bride   at nineteen
calls the "bluebird of happiness"
her older husband   always at the store

*my beautiful dove was compelled to be alone….Is it a wonder she
began to be nervous, began to worry about her relatives & friends…
left behind in Germany.*

They named her condition "nervous prostration"

*I should have known better to take an almost
schoolgirl out of a foreign country & bring her where everything was
foreign to her…We began to seek medical aid….*

The bluebird of happiness stayed in the teapot

III.

Often dropped off to visit grandparents
this ritual   by myself listening   to the Victrola
"Little Red Riding Hood"   could recite every line   make myself
sit still until   "the better to eat you with my dear"
shrieking   race to the kitchen   to Grandma's arms

Every time I visit   jump out of the car
my little legs fly-away coat   as fast as
top of the steps blackdress oldladyshoes greyhairbun
earlobeselongatedearrings   smile widening arms outstretched
her laughter

Italicized narrative portions from Xeroxed family copy of handwritten memoir by Herman Wilk, dated Dec. 7, 1938 Tucson, Ariz.

Italicized list of Wilk relatives known to have been murdered during the Second World War taken from PDF emailed to Karen Klein from Dr. Immanuel J. Wilk, b.1920- d.2017.

Shower

Did they speak when they went in
thinking they were only going
to get clean? Trying to shake off
the residue of last night's dream
while I shower to wake up, I dimly
sense murmuring fear no words
just sounds   jumble of voices.
Did they have a chance for farewells
before Zyklon B silenced language?

I need this memory-- a long ago
time in deep summer, the trees
outside the bathroom window
in full leaf, sunshine plashing
on the bright tiles, the water warm,
plentiful. I luxuriate in my body,
making it clean to meet my lover,
the shower a prelude to adventure
not annihilation.

Journal 2017: Cordoba

I could not be
in Spain for the first
possibly only
time and not see
Cordoba, center of La Convivencia
keeper of centuries' scars

visit the cramped Jewish Quarter
where Maimonides was born
where a small plaza is named for him
where ghetto inhabitants
were denied egress
from dark til dawn
where a small upstairs room
once served as a synagogue
bare walls frame
empty space

marvel at the Mezquita
the Great Mosque
worship jewel of the Moors
rulers of the Iberian peninsula
its enormous stone arches
siena and cream
once open to the air
echo across acres
its pillars rise to sky's breath

1236 Anno Domini
a broken connection
Mezquita's stone arches   enclosed
imposed in their center
the windowless Cathedral
fortress of Catholic Spain
its airless walls later hung
with Baroque agonies
tormented flesh
bloody with martyrdom

in its dizzying maze of small rooms
I can't breathe
nowhere to rest

tourists herded
through endless displays
gold objects that smell of power
the revolting giant statue
of the porcine bishop
surrounded by gilded putti
their tiny penises
playful

view the Casa
built for sensual joy
a Muslim ruler for his beloved
I breathe pleasure
gardens surrounded by
flowing streams

imagine celebratory evenings
castanets and wine dance
in the Great Hall

reincarnated as the courtroom
of the Spanish Inquisition's headquarters
trials for the Conversos
I stand where the condemned stood
too terrified to imagine
their outcome   penitential *auto da fe*
then fire dance at the stake

bath quarters in the Casa
where the beloved
perfumed with ointment
once prepared herself for his
embraces

twisted into torture cells
where the body   joy's source
transformed into excruciating
agony
to be now, here, a tourist in this place
where I could have been
howling among the condemned heretics
and Jews
our only light
ceiling openings
in the shape of stars

Wild Swans at Waquoit

I.

Yeats saw them a century ago
at Coole near Connemara.
Their sudden, wheeling flight
stirs him to sadness—all had changed
since his first count of them,
years replete with personal grief
and political tumult.

     I see them
at Sage Lot Pond, an inlet of the Bay.
Their serene beauty slumbers on the water,
 their oval backs glisten ivory,
 sun on their silky surface.

Walking between Waquoit Bay
and Vineyard Sound, a watery world
on both sides, my path bounded by
bayberry, beach plum, juniper, cedar,
I breathe in a bit of paradise.

     Glaciers melt
in the far north; chunks break off. The force
of water no longer icily encased cascades
into swirls of ever rising oceans;
the water where wild swans sleep
no longer an invitation,
but a threat.

II.

Cloud cover drains the landscape
of color. Fewer swans yesterday
at Sage Lot Pond. Those there
no longer in repose. Their necks
elongated periscopes
strain to see what's coming.

On our other coast, my cousin,
age ninety-seven, is dying.
A refugee from Nazi Storm Troopers,
he sees his life spiral back with televised
images of torchlit parades
that illumine faces shining
with old hatred
and hears the chant "Jews will not
replace us."

Sage Lot Pond empty today,
its opaque surface undisturbed.
From nowhere, a murmuration
of dark birds explodes into the open sky,
glides on gusts, rides in waves
of panic and purpose, then settles
into a stand of juniper and cedar,
only to lift again, a massive
funnel of tree swallows that widens
into a ceaselessly moving circle
and disappears.

gut knowledge

Long distance phone call: my ninety-seven year old
cousin, a week before his death, tells me he wants
his home care aides to come earlier. I don't understand
why nine in the morning isn't early enough. His explanation,
hesitant, moves step by reluctant step. "I had an accident…
I don't always make it…[the shamed last words nearly
inaudible] to the toilet." I wince, mindful of nursing home
residents who lie, helpless as infants, all night
in their soiled bedclothes and sheets until workers
come in the morning to clean them up.
At least my cousin is at home.

Years before, also at home, near dawn my partner loses
control of his intestines, the hospital bed, brought in
and placed next to our bed, filled with unstoppable waste.
Panicked and alone, I plead, cry, beg him to help me,
to be my partner in this too, respond to my touch, roll
on one side-- I need to clean you, change the bedding--
then roll back, then roll to the other side. He does.
We finish the task together. Two dawns later, he dies.

Five years later, in a different house,
a different bed, another dawn, I wake to an uncomfortable
urge

gut knowledge
the meaning
of old

Planted

Two summers gone since Jim became ash.
The hunter green square box
so heavy
and him
so skinny
so wasted.
Some of him scattered from kayaks into the clam-filled bay.
Some of his cremated bones honor the earth,
    Adamah, our birth mother,
intermingle with the soil under my newly planted
    Turtleheads
      chosen because they can survive
    Joe Pye Weed
      because weeds grow better than cultivars.
They're natives and perennials and will come back next season
and the next and the next because that's what perennials do.

But I made the wrong choices.
Unaware, I brought home swamp plants
who like to keep their feet wet
and put them in a sandy, dry soil.
They won't come back next year.

Sequoia

your name   mellifluous
saying it opens my mouth
your old growth forest dwarfs
my imagination

only once did I step into
your redwood home   look skyward
to your soaring presences   your roots shallow
but widely intertwined   nurturing one another

pressing my entire body
against yours   without thinking
my voice called out to you
'Grandfather'

never visited you again
never again touched your strength
but I have kept you within me
'Grandfather'

October Rose
for Erica and David

you who began life in a squingey pot
now needs two support trellises

what are you doing here?

you had your June glory   stunning
yellow-gold   apricot   pink-blushed petals
colorflood   by the back porch

September splendor a bit less profusion
ah, your color still eyeshocks us breathless

bloom finished   careful pruning
scissor cuts to next leaf   five ovals
not three   bare twigs   seasonal waiting

against Van Gogh's encompassing blue October sky
a single bud at your tip-top invades
recalls June sheens   September radiance

its pointed tip   thrust directly up
defiant middle finger message

whenever anything's over
it's never really ever
over

road to nowhere/and everywhere

Commitment to Poetry

When did you make one, the reading's organizer asked.
I never made one.   Poetry made a commitment to me.

Riding Amtrak from Massachusetts to Virginia
stared out the window as bleak turned to moist

concrete cracks of ruined industries filled with weeds
tree buds   more bush buds   more budding

I was in a dance with Spring rushing toward me
at X-press speed   rendez-vous with flowers in D.C.

Poetry pulled words out of me into crickets' rhythmic iteration
and two notes of an out-of-time bird

when the warm darkness of Autumn's equinox drew me alone
out into deep night's welcome   scant raindew on my face

I melt into it.

My Orion

I watched and I waited for you
    waited and watched
as August slid into September
domino days fall onto each other
    woke at 4:30am
    hunting for you the Hunter
    you never came

Futon under the loft window
I stare directly up at only sky
    pre-dawn of the Equinox
    there you were
    right on time
startling   central   aggressive

Your four stars separate the clouds
    your diagonal belt
    an arrow's thrust
the cosmos your hunting grounds

On our axial planet eaten by ravenous fires
    floods gulp rooftops
    earth burps lava
virus and pollution spoil the air

With Nature's old calendar outdated
    it cheers me to know
    from your appearance
        Orion
the order of the universe still holds.

Thermometer

Everything is soft now.
The afternoon light   tender not dull
takes on a pinkish cast
mauve   the color of elderly ladies.
It's nap time.

Twilight will bring the chill
advance guard of fierce December
darkness.   We have been warned.
Hibernate.

But we are not bears.
We illuminate night   reject its embrace.
Awake, we crave candle flames
bonfires   flares
any hot redness we can hurl
up   into   against the icy dark.

Ignored, the animal inside us shivers.

When We Could Still Go Home

snow fingers
clutch the jagged rock wall
along Mass Pike
their glazed white residue
defiant in the sun's relentless
glare
which striates through dense
very tall   very thin   very bare
trees
a stockade fence
threaded with the light
of late afternoon flooding
barren
snow-dotted farmers' fields
leaching out the
loneliness
so deep you can't bear it

but there may be a warming
fire
on the hearth
when you get there
maybe an aged
whiskey
worth the trip

going home
the rusted metal
of old bridges

The Rite of Spring

I.

the forest is fragrant   damply fresh that morning
ribbons of our laughter
run ahead of us
twine around tree trunks
Yoshi and I weave and duck among them
separate to return to a giggling embrace
heading for the clearing

welcome signs of spring in the branches' new buds
firm and small like my nipples
my monthly bloods have started
so have Yoshi's
we are no longer children, but maidens
only maidens are allowed to dance
to become the Chosen One, an honor
who will be chosen
a mystery

soon my father will find a husband for me
my nipples will darken   my breasts fill with milk
'til then I'm a maiden and today I will dance

II.

brightly colored ribbons in our long braids
twirl in the wind
we maidens walk slow-paced
behind village elders with somber face
once in the clearing they form a large circle

order us inside it
command us to dance

we link hands   make the circle of maidens
Yoshi's strong grip wrenches my wrist
our steps quicken
then faster   & faster   & faster & faster&faster
stomps of the elders echo beat of our feet
arms tugging and tugged
air we gulp filled with sounds of our panting
the elders surround us   tighten our circle
crushing and crushed
body on body

torn from our circle
into the embrace of the elders
Yoshi   her screams

I was not the Chosen One.

This poem is based on a video of The Joffrey Ballet's version of Sergei Diaghilev's Ballet Russe performance in Paris, May 29, 1913 of Stravinsky's le sacre du printemps choreographed by Vaslav Nijinsky.

Spring

When the ice finally breaks
all the images of restraint give way
surely the Norse warriors   winter-trapped
in their tribal enemies' mead hall
feel desire's fire for their dragon-prowed ship
move their feet apart   balance's
stance   readies for the swell
the water builds its sullen resistance
eyes narrow   shoulders and legs become
the rhythm of the oars

Their scop, *Beowulf's* shaper, nailed it
foamy-necked floater most like a flier
the double kenning   one for boat
                           the other bird
both swiftly move through water and air
                        without wings
                        with wings
both escape the soil of earth
while fire unconquerable
consumes the mind in desire's flame
for the watery road to nowhere
and everywhere

Italicized line from the Seamus Heaney translation of Beowulf

'the green fuse'
for Dylan Thomas

unraked leaves from last fall
crushed by winter snow and wet melt
a compressed mat covering my garden

clean-up delayed by a too late spring
complicated by sturdy green shoots
already shoving their way up & through

the rake's edges too wide to be harmless
so, kneeling, my forearm the rake's handle
my fingers its tines carefully scoop dead leaves

inadvertently brush hosta spears
startled by their powerful thrust
the mutual shock of something live

Acknowledgments

I am grateful to the editors of the following print and online journals in which many of the poems in this book were published, some in earlier versions or with different titles: *Bagel Bards Anthology, Boston Area Small Press & Poetry Scene, Cape Cod Poetry Review,* "Poetry Sunday" in *The Cape Cod Times, Constellations, Free Inquiry, Fusion Magazine, Ibbetson Street, Muddy River Poetry Review, Pudding Magazine, SLANT, The Comstock Review, The Drunken Boat,* "Lyrical Somerville" in *The Somerville Times, Wilderness House Literary Review,* and to the following venues in Massachusetts in which some of my poems which are included in this book, some in earlier versions or with different titles, were performed with the teXtmoVes collaborative: Arts at the Armory, Somerville, *Boston Poetry Festival* at the Community Church of Boston, The Dance Complex, Cambridge, *We Create* at Hibernian Hall, Roxbury, *Selmadanse* at the Newton Arts Festival, Newton Highlands, North Hill Retirement Community, Starlight Square, Cambridge, Third Life Studio, Somerville.

I have been the fortunate recipient of much kindness and support from the community of poets and friends.

I am grateful to Joan Houlihan and Rusty Morrison at the Colrain Manuscript Conference where I learned strategies for shaping a manuscript. This book is not the same manuscript I brought to Colrain a few years ago -- some poems have been retained in revised form --, but has benefited much from that learning and later from Joan's one-day workshop and her cogent suggestions on specific poems.

Gratitude to Sean Singer for his challenging class, "Thinking Through Poetry," for his helpful kindness in our most recent exchanges, and for his gift to all of us of "The Sharpener" online.

Thanks to dear friend and dancer/choreographer extraordinaire, Joanie Block who, when I asked her to recommend someone who did not know me and had never read my poems to be a fresh eye on my then most recent manuscript(2021), led me to Bernard Horn whose intelligent, critical reading gave me the impetus to redo, reshape, rethink that manuscript which led to this book. Many thanks to Bernie.

Although *This Close* does not contain any formal haiku, it was in my daily haiku practice that writing poetry begin. I am grateful to Raffael deGruttola who upon seeing my haiku gently told me I had never written one, brought me into the Boston Haiku Society where I learned how. On reading some of my contemporary lyric poems, Raffael astutely noted how much my haiku practice has influenced my writing.

Thanks, too, to Olga Broumas who, in her informal Brandeis seminar into which I came by a misunderstanding, first gave me confidence that I might actually write poetry.

Heartfelt thanks to poet/editor Doug Holder whose unfailing support, promotion, and publication of my work has made all the difference; more thanks for his generous support for poets, for creating and sustaining a community of poets and poetry magazines and for being a teXtmoVer.

Enormous gratitude to other dear poet friends: beloved Samm

Carlton who reads and comments on every poem I send her; to poet/editor Nina Rubenstein Alonso whose critical acumen and friendship are invaluable; to jazz poet Elizabeth Gordon McKim, my partner in crime and teXtmoVes; to dearest Debra Cash a valued longtime friend and public supporter of my work in poetry and dance; to Kathleen Spivak who generous praise lifts my spirits; to dancer/choreographer Kelley Donovan who always asks me to read at the Speakeasy; to poet/dancer Melissa Buckheit for information on publishing poems and body issues; to poet/writers Milton Teichman and Sharon Leder who listen to and read my poems as we meet in creative friendship and invited me to read at their Cape Salons; to Jack Klaus for sharing poems and letters.

Special thanks to wonderful poet, dear friend Judson Evans who started our weekly Friday morning crit group and who performs his vibrant poetry with teXtmoVes, and to Sam Sheffer, part of Friday's group; their intelligent, unsparing critical comments and unwavering support have made my poems better.

I am blessed to belong to two other groups: many thanks to Steeple Street Poets and to Christina Laurie who first introduced me to them; my poems have benefitted from their careful, critical attention at our monthly meetings. Great gratitude to the Bagel Bards for supportive camaraderie weekly, for poems, laughter, controversial arguments-none better.

Because a few of the poems that have been performed are included in different form in this book, I want to include thanks to those who have danced them 2016-2021: Audrey Albert King, Katrina Obarski, Teresa Fardella, Joanie Block, Julie Leavitt, Marian Ingegneri, Jim Banta, Julie Becker, Ofri Rieger, Katrine Gagnon, Kelley Donovan, Tomomi Imai, J. Michael Winward, Sean Murphy and to those members of my family who have watched performances.

There are friends who sustain poets, those who, when I have asked to sit still and listen to my poem have done so. I am grateful to Robin Dash, Elizabeth Michelman, Isvel Bello, to the best barflies: Pam Allara, Joyce Antler, Erica Harth who brainstormed book titles; to those Radcliffe Classmates who voted on cover art; to my sister, Judith Alban-Wilk, to my daughter and poetry executor who read the entire penultimate manuscript, Martha Klein, and to the memory of Jimmy Garabedian who made our before dinner scotches and patiently listened, curbing his natural acerbic comments.

I am grateful to Ibbetson Street Press, to the editor Doug Holder and to artist, designer, Steve Glines whose magic put it all together.

About the Author

KAREN KLEIN'S creative thread runs through many forms: poetry, dance, visual art. After retiring from Brandeis faculty, she returned to modern dance, performing for 15 years with Prometheus Elders and 8 years with Across the Ages Dance. In 2011-12, she performed in Prometheus Dance production of Desiderare; her poetry provided the verbal structure. She has published poems nationally and internationally in both haiku and modern lyric forms in print and on-line journals, in anthologies and newspapers.

In 2016 she founded teXtmoVes, a poetry/dance collaborative with past performances in art galleries, public libraries, Hibernian Hall, The Dance Complex, the DeCordova Museum and Starlight Stage. A member of Steeple Street Poets and BagelBards, she currently works with choreographer Sean Murphy in dance theater productions. *This Close* is her first book of poems.

Karen Klein's **This Close** is a beautiful read, the poems ranging widely in mood and tone. Her partner's painful, fatal illness includes a grieving awareness of her own body registering "the meaning of old." Parthenon presents an excited "First time tourist," while Tribal Tongues is playful about Yiddish that enriches "…my tribe/those meshugena enough to make poems." Commitment to Poetry describes her mysterious process of vision: "Poetry made a commitment to me…pulled words out of me…scant rain dew on my face…I melt into it," an engaging, sensitive collection.

— **Nina Rubinstein Alonso,** author, *Riot Wake*, editor, *Constellations a Journal of Poetry and Fiction*

"This Close," is a late-life collection of poems by the multi-talented Karen Klein. This brilliant woman, who has achieved so much in other areas of life, both artistic and academic, now turns to a poetry-memoir form to reflect on further aspects. The author is always thoughtful and deep. But it is her honesty and playful intelligence that make "This Close" sparkle and leap off the page!

— **Kathleen Spivack,** author, *"With Robert Lowell and His Circle: Plath, Sexton, Bishop, Kunitz et al"*. University Press of New England, *"Unspeakable Things,"* Knopf.

With the line and volume of a sculptor, the kinetic embodiment of a dancer, and precise sensory detail of the haiku poet, "When you split wood,/ one side knows/ it belongs to what it has lost," Karen Klein's new collection gathers a life's deep experience in a cresting wave. With an ear shaped by the dissonances between her family's Jewish and Norwegian voices, and an innate curiosity that takes nothing on its word, Klein creates a language for desire that veers from the poignant "first big hug/ our octopus arms/ touch through layers" to the lacerating "The Angel held her flaming/ sword barring my way back to yesterday's me./ Now in danger forever, someday/ I would walk into it naked." This Close exactly measures a distance to memory, history, art, as well as to existential cruxes: "gut knowledge/ the meaning/ of old"—and psychic lightning strikes: "We didn't know what was coming./ We didn't know we would drown. / We will drown" that Lee Gurga speaking of the caesura of haiku describes with the metaphor of the gap in a spark plug. That charge leaps from a playful aside about children's annoyance with 'naps' to a chilling anecdote of adolescent confrontation with annihilation: "I fell asleep during daylight./ When I awoke, it was night./ To say it was terrifying,/ or to say I was in terror/ implies that I was thinking./ I wasn't thinking./ It was thinking me./I knew I would die./ I knew I would wake in the dark."

— **Judson Evans**, Berklee College of Music, author, *Chalk Song* with Gale Batchelder and Susan Berger-Jones

Made in United States
North Haven, CT
14 July 2022